Build a Neighborhood Library

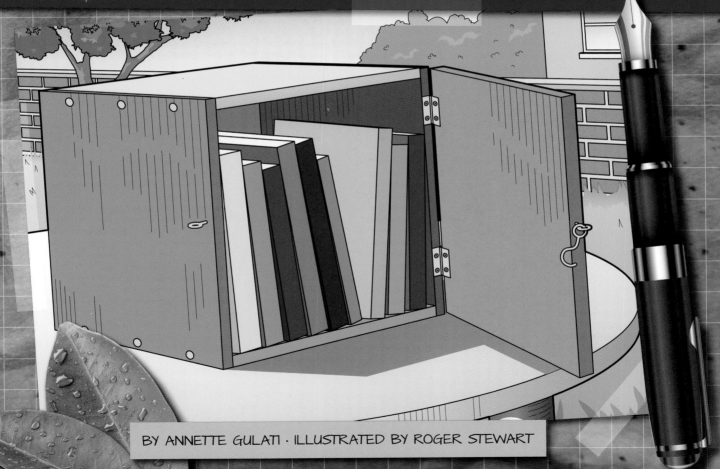

BY ANNETTE GULATI · ILLUSTRATED BY ROGER STEWART

Published by The Child's World®
1980 Lookout Drive · Mankato, MN 56003-1705
800-599-READ · www.childsworld.com

Acknowledgments
The Child's World®: Mary Swensen, Publishing Director
Red Line Editorial: Editorial direction and production
The Design Lab: Design

Photographs ©: Alejandro Rivera/iStockphoto, 5; Steve
Debenport/iStockphoto, 6; iStockphoto, 7, 8

Design Elements: JosephTodaro/Texturevault; Shutterstock Images

ISBN 9781503807907

LCCN 2015958142

Printed in the United States of America
Mankato, MN
June, 2016
PA02301

ABOUT THE AUTHOR

Annette Gulati is a freelance writer and children's author living in Seattle, Washington. She has published stories, articles, essays, poems, and activities in numerous magazines, newspapers, and anthologies. She also writes educational books for children.

ABOUT THE ILLUSTRATOR

Roger Stewart has been an artist and illustrator for more than 30 years. His first job involved drawing aircraft parts. Since then, he has worked in advertising, design, film, and publishing. Roger has lived in London, England, and Sydney, Australia, but he now lives on the southern coast of England.

Contents

CHAPTER ONE

From Trees to Paper to Books

Books tell us stories. They teach us new things. They make us laugh and cry. We can buy books at the store or download them onto our computers or tablets. We can also borrow them from the library. Books are great for us! But what about for our environment?

Millions of books are made in the world every year. All paper books start as trees. The United States cuts down millions of trees each year to make books. Most of the time, new trees are planted to replace those that are cut down. But other times, more trees are cut down than are planted. This hurts animals and the environment. Trees store a gas called carbon dioxide. Trees that are cut down can no longer take in this gas. Carbon dioxide is bad for nature. It increases the rate of **climate change**.

Turning trees into paper can also be harmful. Factories use chemicals when they make paper. Those chemicals can add to **pollution** in our air and water. Making ink to put on books' pages can also add to pollution. After the printed pages are made into books,

E-books do not take up any paper.

they need to be shipped to stores. The ships, planes, and trucks that move books make pollution, too.

Some **publishers** are doing their part to help the environment. Many are now making books out of recycled paper. Some are using only paper made from certain forests and trees. Others are not using paper at all. They're making e-books. There are things we can do to help the environment, too.

CHAPTER TWO

Helping Communities

Using a library is one way to help the environment. At libraries, you can borrow a book instead of buying one. You can also borrow magazines, newspapers, and audiobooks. When you borrow a book instead of buying it, you save trees and prevent pollution.

But the environmental benefits are just one good thing about libraries. Libraries are special places in our communities. You can meet new people at the library or do homework with friends. You can use computers to study or

Libraries allow you to take home books for a certain amount of time.

to play games. Libraries sometimes show movies. They also offer classes and have guest speakers.

Libraries serve communities in many ways.

We can thank a businessman named Andrew Carnegie for many of our libraries. When Carnegie was young, he wanted to use his neighborhood library. But it charged money to borrow books. Carnegie couldn't afford the cost. So he wrote a letter to a newspaper. He said every child should be able to use a library. The library changed its rule. It started to lend books. Carnegie later became one of the richest people in the United States. He knew libraries were important. He thought people could use them to learn and to become successful. When he got older, Carnegie gave away millions of dollars. The money helped build more than 2,500 libraries around the world.

CHAPTER THREE

Big and Little Libraries

Libraries come in all shapes and sizes. The largest library in the world is in Washington, DC. The Library of Congress has more than 36 million books and other printed items. But a library doesn't have to be big to be useful.

In 2009, a man named Todd Bol built his own library in Hudson, Wisconsin. Bol's library was different. He built

The Library of Congress was started in 1800.

a tiny model of a schoolhouse. He made it out of recycled materials. He filled it with books. He placed it in his front yard. He added a sign that said, "Free Books." The little library was a **tribute** to his mother, who was once a teacher.

Soon, Bol met Rick Brooks. The two men started a company called Little Free Library. Their **motto** was, "Take a book, return a book." Bol and Brooks wanted to give people a chance to trade good books. They also wanted to bring people together. Their goal was to build as many libraries as Andrew Carnegie. Today, there are more than 32,000 Little Free Libraries. They can be found in 70 countries. There are Little Free Libraries in all 50 states.

Why would someone want to build a neighborhood library? Like Bol, many people enjoy sharing books with others. They like meeting neighbors, and they also care about Earth. They think it's important to reuse old books. Many people also reuse materials to make their libraries.

CHAPTER FOUR

Building a Neighborhood Library

Do you love books? Do you enjoy making things? Or do you want to help the environment? Then this is the project for you!

Read through all the steps before starting your project. Gather your materials. Use as many recycled items as possible. Find old scrap pieces of wood. Reuse nails. Use leftover paint from other projects. Then, find a flat surface to work on. An old table or workbench works well. Ask an adult for help when you need it. Let's get started!

WHERE TO PUT YOUR LIBRARY

Before you start making your library, think about where you might put it. You can set it on your porch. You can put it on a small table in your yard. Maybe a neighborhood park or school has a good spot. Make sure you get permission before you put your library in a public place.

MATERIALS

- ☐ 4 pieces of .5-inch (1.3 cm) thick **plywood** cut to 10 x 10 inches (25 x 25 cm)
- ☐ Wood glue
- ☐ Pencil
- ☐ 20 1.5-inch (3.8 cm) nails
- ☐ Hammer
- ☐ 2 pieces of .5-inch (1.3 cm) thick plywood cut to 10 x 11 inches (25 x 28 cm)
- ☐ Ruler
- ☐ 2 **hinges**
- ☐ 4 to 6 .5-inch (1.3 cm) nails
- ☐ Sandpaper
- ☐ Old rag or cloth
- ☐ Drop cloth or newspaper
- ☐ Paint
- ☐ Stir stick
- ☐ Paintbrush
- ☐ Hook and eye set
- ☐ Varnish or sealant

STEP 1: Take two pieces of 10-inch (25 cm) square plywood. Stand one upright and lay one down. Add a thin line of wood glue down one edge of the upright piece. Be careful not to use so much that it drips. Press the glued edge down onto the plywood that is lying down. The upright piece should stand along the edge of the piece lying down. Together, they should form an L shape.

STEP 2: Add glue to an edge of a third piece of 10-inch (25 cm) square plywood. Press the glued edge onto the other side of the L. Now you will have a U shape. Let the glue dry.

STEP 3: Add glue along the top edges of your U shape. Press the fourth piece of 10-inch (25 cm) square plywood to the glued edges. This will create a box shape. Let the glue dry.

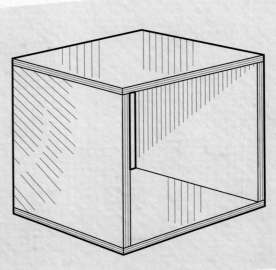

HAMMER TIME

STEP 4: Use nails to make the joints stronger. Stand the box on one side. Take the pencil. Mark three spots along each edge. Carefully hammer a nail into each spot. Do this on each side. You will hammer in 12 1.5-inch (3.8 cm) nails total.

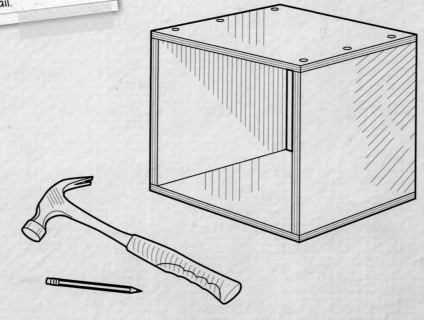

14

STEP 5: Lay down the box so that one of the open sides is facing up. Put glue around all four edges. Line up one of the 10- by 11-inch (25 by 28 cm) pieces of plywood with the edges of your box. Lay it down and press. Let the glue dry.

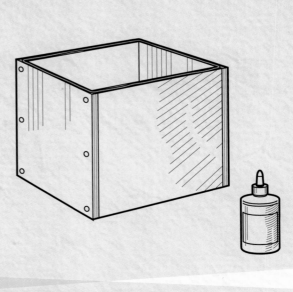

STEP 6: Mark eight spots evenly around the four edges. Carefully hammer a 1.5-inch (3.8 cm) nail into each spot.

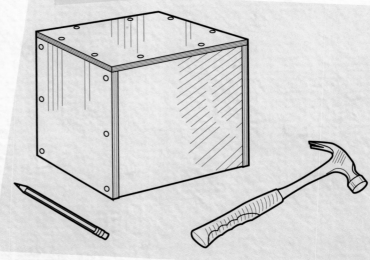

STEP 7: Have an adult help you hold the last piece of wood upright on its 11-inch (28 cm) edge. Place a hinge along the right edge 1 inch (2.5 cm) from the top. Hold the hinge in place and tap .5-inch (1.3 cm) nails into the holes. It might take two or three nails. Add another hinge along the same edge 1 inch (2.5 cm) from the bottom. Nail the second hinge into place.

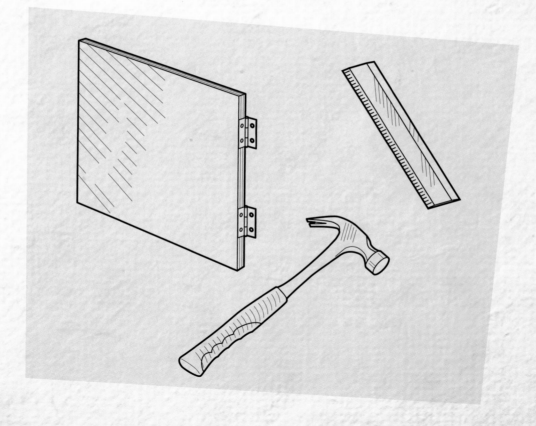

STEP 8: Make sure the open side of the box is facing up. Place the piece of plywood with hinges on top of the box. Have an adult help you hold the door in place. The open halves of the hinges will fasten to the edge of the box. Hold each hinge in place. Tap .5-inch (1.3 cm) nails into the holes.

STEP 9: Use sandpaper to sand your library. Sand the inside and outside. This will make the library smooth. Wipe off the dust with a rag or cloth.

STEP 10: Set your library on a drop cloth or sheets of newspaper. Mix the paint with a stir stick. Use the paintbrush to paint the library. You can paint the outside and the inside. You can also paint with more than one color. But rinse off the brush between using each color. Let the paint dry. Then, add a second coat.

STEP 11: Mark a spot halfway down the edge of the door. Make sure it is the edge without hinges. Screw the hook into place.

STEP 12: Use the hook to pull the door closed. Twist the eye into place on the wall. Make sure the hook can reach it. Latch the hook into the eye.

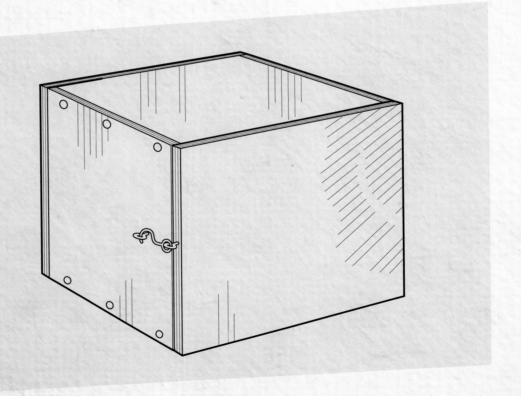

STEP 13: Your library is almost finished. You'll want to protect it from wind, rain, and snow. You can do this with varnish or sealer. Use the paintbrush to seal all sides of your library. Let it dry. Paint a second coat of sealant. This will keep your library looking great.

STEP 14: Place your library in a place for your neighborhood to enjoy.

STOCKING UP

Search for books to fill your library. Do you have any books you no longer read? Ask friends or neighbors for some, too. You could also hold a book drive. Or have a fundraiser, such as a car wash. Use the money you raise to buy books from a thrift store.

GLOSSARY

climate change (KLYE-mit CHAYNJ) Climate change is when there is a big change in the weather over a long period of time. Pollution in the air helps cause climate change.

hinges (HINJ-ez) Hinges are pieces of metal that let a door, lid, or gate swing open and closed. The hinges allow the library's door to open.

motto (MAH-toh) A motto is a saying that announces a person's belief or goal. The Little Free Library's motto is "Take a book, return a book."

plywood (PLYE-wud) Plywood is a piece of wood made by gluing thinner pieces of wood together. A neighborhood library can be made with plywood.

pollution (puh-LOO-shuhn) Pollution happens when dangerous or unhealthy stuff gets into the water or the air. Throwing trash in a river is one form of pollution.

publishers (PUHB-lish-urs) Publishers are companies that create and print books, magazines, or newspapers. Publishers can use recycled paper to make books.

tribute (TRIB-yoot) A tribute is a gift given to show respect for someone. Bol built a schoolhouse library as a tribute to his mother.

TO LEARN MORE

In the Library

De Capua, Sarah. *Andrew Carnegie*. Ann Arbor, MI:
Cherry Lake, 2008.

Elliot, Marion. *Recycled Craft Projects for Kids: 50 Fantastic
Things to Make from Junk, Shown Step by Step in over 400
Photographs*. Helotes, TX: EFA Solutions, 2014.

McGuire, Kevin. *The All-New Woodworking for Kids*.
New York: Lark, 2008.

On the Web

Visit our Web site for links about
neighborhood libraries:
childsworld.com/links

*Note to Parents, Teachers, and Librarians:
We routinely verify our Web links to make sure
they are safe and active sites. So encourage
your readers to check them out!*

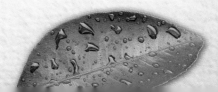

INDEX